NEW CLICHÉS
FOR THE
21ST CENTURY

zuckerisms

Stephen Zuckerman, M.D.

New Clichés for the 21st Century
© 1998 by Stephen L. Zuckerman, M.D. All rights reserved.
ISBN: 0-9672764-0-3

Mitzvah Publishing
2828 Kenwood Isles Drive, C-6
Minneapolis, MN 55408

Editor : Stephanie Ericsson
Desktop publishing design: Bill Herbst
Cover photography: Pamela Thaden
Cover design: Kittelson & Leadholm

To order a copy of this book, contact:

Mitzvah Publishing
2828 Kenwood Isles Drive, C-6
Minneapolis, Minnesota 55408
(612) 874-7825
e-mail: *szuckerman@comcast.net*
or www.mynextie.com

First printing October 1998, 2nd printing May 1999, 3rd printing May 2000
4th printing January 2005, 5th printing September 2007
Printed in the United States of America.

CONTENTS

I .... The Doctor Is In

17 .... On Aging

25 .... On Insanity

31 .... On Idiot Savants

35 .... It's All Just Entertainment

43 .... Everything Is True and So Is the Opposite

49 .... On Procrastination

53 .... On Life and Death

63 .... On Being Human

79 .... The Problem IS the Solution

87 .... On Loneliness, Love, and Gossip

93 .... On Men, Women, and Sex

101 .... It's All Relative(s)

109 .... On Money, Business, and Politics

117 .... What's God Got to Do with It?

123 .... The Pondering Jew

To Dr. Gabriel Kirschenbaum,

whose shoes I wanted to fill
since the age of three years old;

to my many patients,

who helped me fill those shoes;

and, finally, to my children,

for loving me.

A C K N O W L E D G M E N T S

This book could not have been written
without the help of all my patients,
friends, enemies, relatives, and lovers,
who have so openly and generously supplied
me with the nectar of their lives' experience to
help me conceive this book.

Thanks to my editor, Stephanie Ericsson,
who did what I could not, without having
gone crazy.

To my loving parents, who, by not
interfering, gave me the right to be me.

And, lastly, thanks to my woman friend,
Pamela Thaden, *who caused me enough*
angst that I had to write in order to restore
balance in my life.

Deep down inside all of us, there exists a tacit beckoning toward 'something' we must accomplish in our lifetimes if we are to consider our lives fulfilled.

For me, creative writing has been a conscious, lingering summons —one that now demands expression, as my careers in medicine and business have had their turns. The underlying themes of my being, matured and refined by my explorations and collisions with life, have finally found their voice in this book. From now on, I plan to dedicate the years I have left (which, considering the present insurance charts, could be a helluva long time!) to fulfilling my last need before my own life's book closes.

The style of writing I have used in this volume is commonly described as aphoristic. *I chose this style to assert what I feel to be* truths, *in hopes of provoking thought and insight. Since I believe that* everything is true and so is the opposite, *my intent is to tickle, prod, and encourage you, the reader, to think for yourself.*

I hope that you will have as good a time reading the book as I had writing it.

Stephen L. Zuckerman, M.D.

October 1998

ZUCKERISMS

New Clichés for
the 21st Century

The Doctor Is In

When I was a resident in the
emergency room, an intern rushed in
to tell me that he'd just admitted a tapeworm.
I asked him if the tapeworm had come with
the patient or had slithered in on its own.

♦

Doctors view the noncompliant patient
as an encumbrance upon his disease.

♦

When I asked a bald patient who his barber was,
he barked back—'Mother Nature.'

♦

When we give a patient a drug to counteract
the side effects of another drug, we create
a string of lies that cover up the original sin.

The best cure for arthritis is reincarnation.

♦

Cryopreservation and euthanasia are
two sides of the same coin.
Both are interventions on death —
the first wants to hold finality at bay,
while the latter embraces the inevitable.

♦

Up to 90 percent of hypochondriacs
also have 'doctorophilia.'

♦

The podiatrist at our clinic
is considered the Head Foot Man.

HMO studies show that
doctors gain a 30-second savings
per office visit by greeting patients with
'How aren't you?'—a combination of
'How are you?' and 'What's wrong?'
Initially, however, it requires
a two-minute explanation as to why
you changed your standard greeting.

♦

To silence the nagging patient
who is certain that all his doctors
have missed something,
send him to the Mayo Clinic—
his last court of appeal.
Even if he remains incurable,
he'll be much happier.

Engine Failure

Defining heart disease for
the auto aficionado is simple:

The heart is the engine.
Coronary arteries are the fuel lines.

A heart attack happens when
a fuel line clogs and the engine can't get fuel.
Arrhythmia is when the electrical system
malfunctions, so that the accelerator either
runs erratically or stops altogether.

Doctors know only one way
to make money, that is,
to see a patient and charge a nickel.
This is the most inefficient way
to earn a living—by working for it.

♦

From the first day of medical school,
doctors are taught that
patients always lie.

♦

Why isn't the humerus the funny bone?

♦

The first 40 years of life are gratis.
After that, you have to work hard to stay vital.

It has recently been rumored
that lawyers are being paid
surreptitiously by doctors to initiate
malpractice suits against chiropractors.
The rumor was started by chiropractors.

♦

Klutzes on crutches
are known as 'klutches.'

♦

The most important conference
at my medical school was called
'The Death of the Week.'
In order to make it interesting,
it was designed as a guilt-ridden
whodunit thriller, in which a patient's
untimely death ignited a forensic hunt
for the medical miscreant.

To increase 'efficiency,'
HMOs are demanding
that doctors see a patient
every seven minutes.
For doctors to learn
how to develop a rapport
in such a short time,
courses are being taught on
'doctor-patient communication,'
a fancy term for 'instant intimacy.'
Ideally, the courses should be
taught by used car salesmen.

♦

A drug rep once told a cranky doctor,
'If it weren't for the drug companies
you'd be a witch doctor.'
To soothe the enraged doc, the rep
asked for his autograph instead of
his signature on the drug order.

Come nights and weekends,
naturopaths,
chiropractors,
and herbalists
disappear into the woodwork.

♦

X-rated movie theaters
should have two restrictions:
no minors, and no seniors
without a cardiologist's approval.

♦

Doctors go to school for four years
to learn how to write illegibly.
Pharmacists go to school for four years
to learn how to interpret illegible prescriptions.
This is one of the many covert ways
of keeping the patient in the dark.

Internists seek insight.
Surgeons seek to incise.
Administrators seek to devise.
All together, they make a whole.

♦

Someone should patent a chest tattoo
for those who truly do not want
to be resuscitated: *DNR/DNI.*

♦

Someone should write a book
on doctor-patient communication
and title it *How to Treat Patients.*

♦

A urological double-whammy for men
is that as your prostate enlarges,
your penis won't.

I knew a urologist who was formerly
a plumber and a butcher.
He was permitted to take the urology boards
without any further schooling.

♦

There are now winter charter trips
to the desert southwest with a guarantee
of 90 percent sunny days.
The trips are called 'Psoriasis Specials.'

♦

Thanks to Viagra,
tiger testicles and rhino horns
are no longer in great demand
to treat the impotence of rich old men.
This may prove to be the salvation
of these endangered species.

A successful advertisement
above a men's urinal read:
'If you have time to read this sign,
it's time see your urologist.'

♦

A hospital administrator once told a patient
who complained about his hospital charges
that the man should be glad
he was still alive to pay the bill
after having been a patient in that hospital.

♦

I tell my patients that
I practice eternal medicine—
under my care,
they either live forever
or go to their eternal rest.

I told my drunken friend
that alcohol dissolves three tissues:
the brain, the liver, and the testicles.
'Thank heaven that when it dissolves
your testicles,' I informed him,
'it also knocks out your brain,
so you don't care about your balls.
However, when the liver goes, so do you.'

♦

Alcohol and gout go together;
indulge in one and you get the other.

♦

One of my patients complained
that he no longer got morning hard-ons,
so I said, 'Congratulations!
You have outlived your erections!'

I once told a run-down patient,
'You look like three-quarters
of a million dollars.'
His response to me was,
'I don't feel that way,
but I'll take the money anyhow.'

♦

The genius of a cane is that
it gives unstable two-legged people
a third leg to stand on.

♦

I tell overweight patients to
lose 50 pounds and grow a third arm.
When they stare blankly at me,
I say, 'Both would be good for you,
but you're more likely to do the latter.'

My most appreciative patients
are those who come to me just
as their illnesses are about to resolve.
I treat them and take credit for the cure.

♦

I usually tell my patients
who are coughing up sputum that
if the mucous is green or yellow,
we can treat it, but if it's purple,
they'd better jump into the coffin.
Unbeknownst to me, I told this
to a patient who was color blind
and scared him half to death.

♦

I assure my patients that if they remain
under my care, they will live long enough
to get Alzheimer's disease.

15

Eating is irrational.
Thus any rational means
of suppressing it
will always fail.

♦

The sign above my clinic door reads:
The Gates of Health—
Give up disease
All ye who enter here.

♦

Within the next 50 years,
more money will be spent
on cosmetic surgery than
on life-saving procedures.

On Aging

Youth is wasted on the young because
that's where it's supposed to be wasted.

♦

When my patients worry about dying,
I ease their fears by telling them
that dying must be OK, since
my dead patients never complain.

♦

I have a vigorous 90-year-old
male patient from Scottsdale
who is loved by all
the widows in town.
How tables have turned!
I picture him as a single sperm
surrounded by 10,000 aggressive eggs.

Trump Card

I have found that
a comforting comment
for old people who fear cancer is,
'Don't worry, cancer could hardly
grow in your decrepit body.'

While this may seem cruel,
many of these patients
are absolutely convinced
that they have cancer
until they realize that
old age is their trump card.

The physician of a famous historian
with Alzheimer's disease complained
while trying to take his medical history
that his patient was a poor historian.
'That's odd,' I mused,
'he used to be a very good one.'

♦

If only I could remember what I forgot.

♦

Most doctors don't make their livings
from a child being born,
but rather from the aftermarket
created by keeping people alive longer.

Redefining Disease

Nature has designed us to procreate
up until the ages of 40 to 50.
By this time, we've fulfilled Nature's need
for the reproduction of our species.

Therefore, it is incorrect to call illnesses
that occur after the age of 50 *diseases*.
The more accurate term is
advanced maturity conditions,
to signify that ills after age 50
are a result of outliving
our procreative functions.

There is a new form of tennis
for the very senior—it's called triples.
Two seniors play while the third player
recovers from his angina attack.

♦

When my 90-year-old patients ask me,
'How'm I doing, Doc?'
I say,
'You're above ground, aren't you?'

♦

Cars and humans now last twice as long
as they used to—in both cases,
creating a vast aftermarket for
repair and replacement specialists.
The longevity of cars has been improved
by the production of more durable models,
something not yet happening
on the human production line.

Forced Wisdom

Some say we accumulate wisdom with age
because we've experienced the pageantry
of life's ups and downs.

Others say that wisdom is forced on us
by decreasing hormones
and increasing arthritis.

Doctors are limited in their use
of the 'placebo effect' because
that's *spiritual* territory—not *scientific*.

♦

As a doctor, I never say no
to a patient's request for tests
and consultations, no matter how
unsound I think the requests are.
I merely tell the patient
what it will cost him
and ask if he is willing to pay.

On Insanity

A psychiatrist friend of mine
will see only patients
who are crazy enough to see him.

♦

It's no secret that I am
a self-controlled manic.
My friends swear that they have seen me
out of control, but it's only
when I choose to be.

♦

The modern world races to embrace
the practice of instant intimacy.

♦

My friend Maurice is crazy,
but he's working towards being sane.
I don't even try.

Bargain Basement Sanity

There has only been one psychotherapist
I have respected because he guaranteed
meaningful, measurable results
from his therapy.

His bottom line was this:

'Therapy will cost you $10,000
and one hour of your day,
five days a week, for five years.
In that time, your income will
increase in direct proportion to
how much better you will function.
So, I can guarantee that, in the
long run, my fees cost nothing.'

Freud was Shakespeare
with a medical degree.

♦

Maybe there is no such thing as insanity—
maybe it's just breaking the rules.

♦

A member of my family
who thinks that everything is a joke
was sent for seriousness counseling.

♦

Nature provides a universal
definition of mental illness—
if you are hungry and do not seek food,
or cold and do not seek shelter,
or if you have both food and shelter
and don't seek sex, then you are crazy.

Lunacy

Most emergency rooms brace themselves
for a flood of admissions every full moon.
Many experts suspect that the moon creates
tidal changes in the cerebral fluid of the brain,
which may explain bizarre behavior.

Maybe these 'admissions'
should be called *High Tide*.

Would a psychiatrist with depression
be classified as a dual-diagnosis?

♦

The National Institutes of Health's
secret experiment of transplanting brains
was stopped when all 12 people involved
complained postoperatively that
they did not feel like their old selves.

♦

Every revision of the DMS codes
just adds another floor to the
psychiatric Tower of Babble.

♦

Drinking alcohol allows one to enter
the world of spirits. Unfortunately, the
spiritual world is located somewhere else.

On Idiot Savants

All of us are idiot savants.
As such, we should pursue that
which we are best suited for
and avoid the areas in which we are idiots.

♦

God has etched His truth
into the genetic code.

♦

Utopia will be achieved
when most human beings
get to express their true individuality
most of the time.

♦

A definition of frustration:
expecting a frog to fly.

There are those who survive
no matter what happens to them.
Their secret is jumping from
one frying pan into the next
without getting licked by the fire.

♦

I have a friend
who is a genius—unapplied.

♦

One true sign of genius
is the ability to create things
that any idiot could use.

♦

People may be stupid,
but their brains aren't.

It's All Just Entertainment

If we were brutally honest,
we would admit that problems
are the best entertainment we have.

♦

God's dilemma was that
He was bored to hell in Heaven.
That's why He thought up the Universe.

♦

The opposite of efficiency
is entertainment.

♦

When 100 people who believed in
Heaven and Hell were asked
which they thought would be boring,
50 percent said Heaven might be,
none said that Hell would be.

It's not necessarily crazy to hear voices
in your head—it all depends
on how entertaining they are.

♦

If there are two ways
to get to the same place,
most people will take the short cut.
However, the torturous route
is far more entertaining.

♦

According to Damon Runyon, the odds
in life are six to five against you.
Las Vegas is so popular because the odds
are temporarily suspended there.

Writers render in hindsight
what readers seek in foresight.

♦

Both hospitals and Las Vegas
disorient their customers by staying open
24 hours a day, seven days a week.
Las Vegas, however, is more fun
because it has slot machines.

♦

One of my patients was a nude dancer
whose professional nom de plume was
'Gena Tailia.'

♦

The next revision of the Bible
should correct a major problem of
the present version—too little humor.

If God created the Cosmos
out of boredom, then surely
Hollywood is the center of the Universe.

♦

The Polish Jews who immigrated to
New York at the turn of the century
knew that our purpose in life is
to entertain and influence others.
So, they proceeded to found
three great American cities:
Hollywood, Las Vegas, and Miami Beach.

♦

When entertainers and entrepreneurs
can make lots of money
demeaning the President with impunity,
you know you're in a freedom-loving country.

The paranoia of the next generation
is that *this* generation will
solve all of its problems.
Then what purpose would they have?

♦

If there had been TV
during the black plague,
everyone would have committed suicide.

♦

When someone asks,
'How are you?'
You can answer,
'Good—for my age'
or
'Good—for my disposition'
or
'Good—for my religion.'

Evolved Frivolity

It is now broadly accepted that only
10 percent of human effort is necessary
to provide basic food and shelter
for the entire population of the earth.

In another hundred years,
this proportion will be further reduced
to a mere 1 percent.

This means that 99 percent
of all human activity in the future
can then be spent on our so-called
frivolous pastimes, such as
poetry, space exploration, bowling,
and more recreational sex.

Everything Is True
and So Is the Opposite

When I told two friends that I believed that
everything is true and so is the opposite,
one of them immediately objected.
The other said, 'That proves the point.'

♦

To be human is to be perfectly imperfect,
and, therefore, in God's image.

♦

Sometimes your intelligence
tells you one thing
and your brain
tells you something else.

♦

Neither free will nor determinism exists—
only the debate between them.

Choice is the root of all evil.

◆

Try to please everybody
and you will be nobody.

◆

Once you come to believe
that all is true and so is the opposite,
you have achieved the ultimate tolerance.

◆

He who hesitates is lost,
but look before you leap.

◆

If everything is true as well as the opposite,
then we need the Devil as much as we need God.

To know is to love;
on the other hand,
familiarity breeds contempt.

♦

We are born knowing everything
and we die knowing nothing.
In that, we have fulfilled
our purpose in life.

♦

Once wisdom is attained,
it ceases to have importance.

♦

The term, 'on the other hand,'
is just another way of saying
'Everything is true and so is the opposite.'

Which Way to the Center of the Universe?

The way Galileo proved that the earth
revolved around the sun was to arbitrarily
select an absolute fixed point in the solar
system—the sun.

This was the simplest way to prove
the Copernican theory that a rotating
earth revolved with other planets around
a central sun. In truth, even Galileo knew
that there is no absolute fixed point
in the solar system.

The Church imprisoned him,
so as to maintain Ptolemy's unruly
and inaccurate geocentrism, which
also maintained that the Church
was the center of the Universe.
In modern terms, this would be
like William of Occam
debating Rube Goldberg.

On Procrastination

By definition, an amoeba cannot
procrastinate, because it is of one mind.

♦

The primary purpose of gray matter
is to deal with gray issues.

♦

We are ambiguous over
what to procrastinate about.

♦

Lots of horses have died of thirst
at the water's edge.

♦

As long as someone else's voice is in your head,
you can't hear your own.

The Collective Brain

Our brains are the paradigm for the
ultimate human society—100 billion
amoebas, all hooked up by electrical
circuitry, continually trying to come
to a consensus.

The Internet mimics this by attempting
to hook up 5 billion brains with
similar electrical circuitry.

There is a simple medical explanation
for procrastination: The brain acts
like a commune of 100 billion cells
hooked up by electrical wiring.
All 100 billion vote on all issues, all the time.
Procrastination occurs when 50 billion
line up on one side of an issue
and 50 billion line up on the other.

♦

Human existence is dedicated to
the art of making choices.

♦

The Devil is the first necessary evil.
Lawyers are the second.
The third necessary evil is Doubt,
which is a first cousin to Procrastination.
Without these evils, there would be
nothing to move us forward.

On Life and Death

Do not attempt perfection,
for it inevitably leads to hopelessness.

♦

The primary cause of death
is life in the first place.

♦

Life is like a horse race—
no matter how much you know about
the horse, past races, or track conditions,
the outcome is always in question.
But if you don't bet, you're not a player.

♦

Pain is no pleasure.

Truth Floats

Humankind is the ultimate judge of
the worth of its leaders.

Common thieves looted and destroyed
the tombs of the Pharaohs,who posed
as gods, and now their words are long
forgotten. Only empty tombs remain.

Not so for the words of Buddha, Lao-
tse, Moses, Jesus, Mohammed, Aristotle,
Plato, Shakespeare, Mozart, Leonardo da
Vinci, and so many others. Their works
have grown and flourished over time.

Famous false prophets inevitably end up
as footnotes in the March of History,
their efforts diminishing with the test
of years. Only the works of those
who bear the burden of truth
survive and deepen with time.

Hope is life's compass
through our voyage in time.

◆

Our most vivid memories are made up
of the unexpected moments of life.

◆

Know how to feed your demons
so that you can keep them at bay.

◆

Don't give up the reins
until the horses are gone.

◆

Happy does not equal content.

Emotional growth, like death,
must be done alone.

♦

The most evocative event of spring
is the reemergence of leaves on the trees.

♦

Don't count your chickens
until after you've eaten them.

♦

Wasting time is a necessary part
of our existence.

♦

Humor is the universal solvent
that dissolves grief and suffering.

History is propelled forward by
the small events of individual lives,
but the direction it takes
is the work of prophets.

♦

Intellectual insemination of open minds
leads to pregnancy of thought.

♦

From dust we come and to dust we return.
Our teeth, however, put up a noble resistance.

♦

Kids of exceptional parents
do not need school at all.
This is the major reason
for the success of alternative schools.

Inseminating the open mind is easy.
The hard part is getting the mind open.

♦

If you think sibling rivalry is rough,
imagine being Siamese twins.

♦

If life is hell,
I want to play the Devil.

♦

Disregard the philosophies
of all dictatorships—
communism, fascism, militarism—
and most religions. They all merely
camouflage the same dogma:
Repress thy neighbor.

Prejudice incarcerates
everyone involved.

♦

Not only does time dilute all suffering,
it dilutes all achievements as well.

♦

The prism of life
turns God's pure white light
into the spectrum of existence.

♦

Nowadays, we live as though the world
will never end and we'll never die.
But Nature puts time limits on our life-spans
so that we will get on with the game.

The dead aren't uptight,
even those who have rigor mortis.

♦

My mother's favorite statement was,
'Peace and quiet—six feet under.'

♦

Ideally, suicide should be committed
with a drug that has no side effects.

♦

The most I can hope for is
that my parents die before me,
and that I die before my children.

On Being Human

It is hard to separate
a fool from his follies.

♦

You can achieve security
through suffering chronic insecurity.
Just try to change someone who is insecure,
then watch him worry about it.

♦

The few people who actually qualify
to throw stones at other people's houses
are the very ones who wouldn't.

♦

Intuition is God's light
seen through the lens
of our own individuality.

Between Battles

Paul was my favorite sparring partner in
business, and I took great pleasure in
poking at his weak points. So, when I
called him to wish him Happy
Hanukkah, naturally, he was suspicious.
'What do you want from me now?'
'Nothing—just to wish you a Happy
Hanukkah.'
'Bullshit. What are you trying
to bug me about now?'
'Maybe the biggest bug of all is
not to bug you about anything.'
He chuckled.

Being 'practical' is often used
to cover up fear.

♦

Don't wish another a fate
that you wouldn't want to befall you.

♦

Indigenous people are not
primitive—they are *primal*.
They exist as close to
the intuitive as possible—
something we 'civilized' folk
are just beginning to rediscover.

♦

Just because I am educated
does not mean that I can't act stupid.

Acceptance

Our human destiny is the acceptance
that we embody the mind of God,
and that the universe is the physical
and spiritual embodiment of love.

Anger is a wonderful thing
if it is pointed in the right direction.

◆

Of 100 individuals offered an opportunity
to return to the Garden of Eden,
98 refused. The other two
were arrested by psychiatrists.

◆

Each person lights his own lamp
to burn in its own fashion.

◆

People who refuse to stop drinking
and driving should be legally required
to change their license plates to DWI-#____
(*fill in the blank for the number of previous arrests*).

The Price of Honor

Years ago, a counselor was fired at the
Westchester day camp where I worked.
He claimed he needed bus money
to get back to New York City,
but nobody volunteered a dime,
because he was a known liar.

When I loaned him the money,
he swore profusely that he'd repay me.
This was obviously unlikely,
but I told him that five dollars was
a cheap price to buy back his honor.

So far, I haven't been paid back.
But then, my life isn't over.
And, hopefully, neither is his.

Alcohol is known as an excellent solvent.
My drunken friend proves it over and over—
only a couple of ounces dissolve his social graces
and expose the beast beneath.

◆

Hypocrisy is a means
of massaging reality.

◆

Don't tell the truth all the time.

◆

The reason people plan for the future
is to relieve their anxiety about the present.

◆

Egomania is when a grain of sand
thinks that it's a meteorite.

Divine Wrong

God's message was transmitted through
the Jews, Essenes, Gnostics, Sufis,
and Buddhists—humble, common
people who were led by God's word.
They were compassionate equals
to their fellow humans.

Many claimed divine right, however,
—kings, emperors, moguls, and other
supposed superiors to the masses—
and ruled by armed oppression.

History confirms that humankind will
always overthrow what is forced on us,
for obvious reasons.

I have a photographic memory,
but, every now and then,
I forget to put film in the camera.

♦

There are four reasons not to die:
1. You're afraid to die;
2. You're enjoying life;
3. You don't want your estranged
   spouse to have fun frittering
   away your hard-earned estate;
4. You have to answer the phone.

♦

Great individual acts and thoughts
may seem of themselves to change
the course of history, but it is only
the acceptance from the sea of humanity
that sustains them.

A phone call is like fishing:
you don't know who's on the other end
until you reel it in.

♦

The best formula to motivate humans
is three carrots and a stick.

♦

Manipulation is when you intend harm;
influence is when you intend good.

♦

Change comes either from
the mirror or from the wall.
If insight doesn't change you,
the hard wall will.

We deny our intuitive knowledge of the future
so we can enjoy the present.

♦

There are four things that
people are willing to spend money on:
food, shelter, sex, and God.

♦

My contemporaries who develop
incurable diseases buoy my spirit,
frighten me, and sadden me—
all at the same time.

♦

The healing arts provide the most direct
occupational means of expressing
our innate human desire to help others.

Forgiveness

Freud gave us permission to blame
our parents for our upbringing.

Science also tells us that we can blame
our parents, but only for the genes
they passed on to us.

Neither has solved anything.

So, either we *blame* our parents,
and ultimately become them.
Or we *forgive* them,
and become our own selves.

My advice to patients who want to change
their lives is to lose weight and stop smoking.
I tell them the best way to do this is to have
a religious experience—an epiphany.
I warn them, however, that it will last
only about six months.

◆

Smoking, alcoholism, drug addiction,
overeating, etc. are now being
categorized under the heading
'Conditions of Human Nature.'
To attempt to eliminate them would be
to attempt to eliminate human nature.

◆

When 90 percent of your conversation
centers around what you have done,
the end is near.

Under Lying Truth

One day, a drunk gave me
the usual line, 'Can you spare
a dollar for a cup of coffee?'

He looked like a decent guy,
so I obliged him, but I felt
compelled to ease his conscience,
so I told him that if he didn't spend
the dollar on whiskey, I'd beat him up.

He hugged me as tears rolled down
his face.

The Problem IS the Solution

Empty stomachs lead to open minds.

♦

Near-death experiences
are the most rewarding.

♦

To cure my son's lackadaisical attitude,
I took him to a compulsive-obsessive
clinic for treatment. I figured that
if they could cure the disease,
maybe they knew how to cause it.

♦

To be successful,
one must be prepared for trouble,
and like it.

Being an individual guarantees
that you'll make enemies.
The idea is to keep the list
as short as possible.

♦

In the physical universe,
the only path to Truth
is through trial and error.

♦

It's not that the flea doubts
the good intentions of the elephant,
but, rather, that he rightly perceives
the consequences of a false move.

♦

I tried to save my ex-girlfriend.
Instead, I was saved.

Suicides are extremely rare
among those who bet on the ponies
—there's always another race.

♦

A group I work with is made up of people
who have difficulty being close to others.
To solve this problem, I take them
to New York City for a week
to ride the subways during rush hour.
By the end of the week, they're cured.

♦

Ambiguity can either paralyze or motivate.

♦

One of the reasons we are here
is to make mistakes so we can learn.

Death to Me Is Not Living

When I turned 40, I was told that I was dying of cancer. Two months later, the diagnosis was reversed. I didn't have cancer after all.

My doctor, understanding the emotional whiplash I was experiencing, asked what I thought about my circumstances. It made me think.

I told him: 'Now that I am ready to die, I am ready to live.'

In the 1980s,
the great threat to the airlines
was cheap long distance calling.
The airlines have since recovered,
thanks to the torturous 'on-hold' button.

♦

I once ran into a patient
with severe malingeritis.
He required two years off work
to allow the situation to resolve itself.

♦

Without human deviation,
philosophers would be out of a job.

Parallels

Artists use negative space as a powerful
force to define the object of a painting.
The greater the negative space,
the more striking the definition.

In music, the pause, or the absence of
sound, parallels the negative space in art
and intensifies the sound's effect.

The 'silent treatment' in marriage also
parallels this concept. What can one do
in the absence of response but eventually
look at oneself?

Thus, I credit my ex-wife (who is an
artist) with being my *mistress of negative
space.* Without her, I never would have
discovered myself.

The round wheel replaced the square one
mainly because it caused fewer headaches.

♦

The good news on global warming
is that the polar ice caps melting
will raise the sea level and flood
coastal lands mostly owned by the rich,
who can afford to find the solution.

♦

All cities have their faults,
not just San Francisco.

♦

What the earth suffers from
is a bad case of *humanitis*.
Those little buggers are
irritating the hell out of its skin.

On Loneliness, Love, and Gossip

Loneliness started as God's problem.

♦

Ecstasy can be found within oneself
and within others.

♦

When science discovers the loneliness hormone,
it will find that it is universal to all species,
and that love suppresses its blood levels.

♦

Feelings are our yardstick for
measuring what we value.

♦

Loneliness is the main reason we don't completely
eliminate the other members of our species.

Serve Your Self

All behavior is self-serving. We either feed
the ego, or feed the soul.

The most self-serving act we can perform
is to care for another, because it not only
validates our own worth, it also sates
our innate need to belong.

Loneliness is society's glue.

♦

The most powerful tool
for enhancing communication
is the appropriate and frequent use
of the words 'thank you.'

♦

Gossip lowers the loneliness hormone.

♦

The luxury of not changing
is often paid for by solitary living.

♦

Sometimes we would rather die ourselves
than hurt another.

The Importance of Blabber

Gossip has been given a bad name, but it wouldn't exist if it wasn't one of the most intimate forms of communication. In truth, it reduces loneliness very effectively.

Psychotherapy also helps, but it's a distant second to gossip.

It is our human destiny
to search the universe for God,
and to ultimately find Him
within ourselves.

♦

When we lose someone we love,
it is God's love, expressed through
that person, which we actually lose.

♦

Evil is love actively unexpressed.

♦

Those who love to scream that
the world is coming to an end
are really reflecting on their own demise.

On Men, Women, and Sex

Are you man enough to admit
that your wife runs the show?

♦

My 18-year marriage to my ex-wife
was the best of all possible marriages,
considering the characters involved.

♦

Most men put up with their wives
because their wives put up with them.

♦

Nature's fundamental imperative
is that we survive as individuals
so we can reproduce as a species.

It is no wonder that women
deal better with change and trauma.
Every month, they go through
the birth and death cycle.

♦

Marriage, nowadays, is being promoted
mainly by divorce lawyers.

♦

Sticks and stones may break your bones,
but words can break your heart.

♦

I always thought that unisex
meant autoerotism.

The prostitute is the poor man's mistress.

♦

Many men feel that they have
an open wound on their being,
which can be remedied
by applying a woman to it.

♦

Sex, these days, is better safe than sincere.

♦

A surprisingly effective line
I use to meet women is:
'You remind me of my third wife.'
Inevitably, they laugh when they find out
I never had one.

Death over Divorce

The divorce rate in 1900 was so low
because the average life expectancy
was only 47 years.

Why bother divorcing when you'd
probably be dead in a few years?

If you want to have a best-seller,
write a book and call it
Safe Sex, Manual Sex.

♦

It was difficult bringing up
two children and a wife.

♦

Always wake your lover when
the northern lights begin to
dance in the night sky.
Not to do so would be disgraceful.

♦

Men are unfaithful by nature,
because they're basically
complex sperm-delivery systems.

The reason nuns and priests
don't have human lovers
is so that they can better hear
the voice of their spiritual beloved.

♦

A best-selling video for men
would be one hour of unedited
women's locker room talk
on what women really think
about men.

It's All Relative(s)

Relativity may intrigue physicists,
but relatives are the mainstay of the masses.

♦

I arranged for my elderly father to sit
in Seat 8A on a flight leaving from Gate 8A
—that way, he had less to forget.

♦

When I was two and a half years old,
my mother let go while teaching me
to swim in the ocean. After that,
there was nothing to rebel against.

♦

When I first met Hal,
he acted like a three-year-old.
In the last ten years he's matured.
Now he acts like a five-year-old.

'It's All Relatives.'

QUOTE FROM THE EINSTEIN
OF PAPUA NEW GUINEA

During my tour of duty in the Truk
Islands, I read a government study that
stated that unemployment among Truk
natives was an astounding 95 percent.
By this point in my tour, I understood
the tribal nature of Trukese society and
their economy, which was based entirely
on fishing and harvesting planted and
native crops.

According to the study, the only jobs
the Trukese held were in schools, hospitals
and a jail—all U.S. government projects.
In Trukese culture, however, these jobs were
meaningless. Schools were unnecessary,
since all their children were raised by
dozens of relatives who taught them

everything required for survival on the island. Hospitals were virtually useless, since native medicine was readily available. Furthermore, jails were a joke to the Trukese who knew each other so well, and gossiped so much, that the entire village knew long before any crime was committed. Ergo—crime was virtually nonexistent. But since the Trukese are a playful people, they humored the U.S. government by accepting these jobs.

In truth, the 5 percent of 'employed' Trukese were being paid to pretend to work, while the 95 percent who were unemployed actually kept the society safe, healthy, and fed.

By our standards, they were hopelessly unemployed. By their standards, unemployment was an unknown concept.

Somebody

Recently, my elderly aunt told me a story
that my father told her 55 years ago.
She was so impressed by it that she
remembered it, verbatim, but, for
some odd reason, she related it to me
only many years later.

She said that one day when I was three,
my father heard me speaking out loud in an
empty room. When he asked me who I was
talking to, I answered, 'To somebody.'

He then asked, 'Who is that somebody?'
to which I replied, 'That somebody I am
talking to knows who he is.'

I have no recollection of the incident,
but to hear the voice of my youth filled me
with wonder. That my aunt remembered it
endeared her even more to me.

I tried to hate my ex-wife,
but I ended up
making her a relative.

♦

My dyslexic cousin always
brags about his high Q.I.

♦

When my girlfriend asked me
what my relatives in Florida
thought of her, I said:

'They almost always think
highly of others because they
think so little of themselves.'

Her response was: 'How nice.'

My girlfriend's father
and my own father
are both men of the cloth—
hers is a preacher,
and mine is a dressmaker.

♦

My friend George,
to the delight of his associates,
is always spreading false rumors.

On Money, Business, and Politics

We all have our price,
but, in certain instances,
it isn't money.

♦

Lawyers and accountants should print
their opinions on gray paper, because
they always state their opinions
with ifs, ands, or buts.

♦

The highest form of slavery
is owning your own business.

♦

The specter of prosperity rolls
ominously over the simple life.

Devil's Advocates

Insurance companies are the
most advanced religious thinkers.

One hundred years ago, they
completely eliminated the Devil
by declaring that all disasters
—volcanoes, hurricanes,
tornadoes, and wars—
were 'acts of God.'

America is a free society—
you are free to buy
whatever you can afford.

♦

Still, money better serves those who view it
as a means of obtaining freedom from want
than it does those who use it principally as
a vehicle to accumulate possessions.

♦

A mental disorder unique to stockbrokers
is market-driven manic depression.

♦

Lawyers are a step up for humanity.
In the old days, hit men would simply
break your knees—now lawyers just
break your psyche and wallet.

Today, medical ethicists
are apologists for the new
medical economic policies aimed
at restricting health care costs,
especially in regard to 'end of life' issues.
Twenty years ago, these same ethicists
were positioned 180 degrees
from their present stance.

♦

In daily life,
people see things
in black and white.
In the business world,
they want to see it
in black and red.

♦

A plethora of insurance agents
translates into a dearth of poets.

A foolish company is one
that manufactures keys and then
searches for locks they might fit.

♦

On their own, ignorance, arrogance,
and stupidity are merely dangerous.
But combined, they're a disastrous trio.

♦

Dr. Kevorkian will become
the medical economist
of the coming millennium.

♦

Capitalism built the Internet,
which has taken on a life
of its own and is generating
a post-capitalist world society.

Sleight of Hand

Here is a surefire way to raise money.

Find a half believable concoction of fact
and fiction that concludes that the world
will end if nothing is done. Once *that* is
accomplished, determine the means to
divert disaster and save humanity.

Then, go out and appeal for the money
to accomplish those lofty goals.

This scam has worked for scientologists,
diet book authors, xenologists,
seismologists, environmentalists,
and religious leaders.

The ideal politician is one
with no scruples, morals, or ethics,
who continually bends to the
slightest winds of social opinion.
And this, dear friends, is democracy.

◆

Power and art are both aphrodisiacs,
but of a different ilk.

◆

You know your lawyer and your doctor
are doing their jobs adequately
if you're not in jail or dead.

What's God Got to
Do with It?

'Because I feel like it,'
is God's answer to 'Why?'

♦

God isn't the Creator
who made the Universe,
as if those were two separate things.
God is Creation itself.

♦

When God's truth is revealed,
there won't be a need for missionaries
to spread the word.

♦

God is responsibility
and love—not power.

If an atheist has
an appointment book,
he is not a true atheist.

♦

At the root of monotheism
is the assumption that all is God.

♦

Miracles like walking on water,
levitating, or conjuring up spirits
pale in the face of the
miracle of existence itself.

♦

For God, creation
is transformation.

Science is what and how—
God is why.

♦

The reason God made the world round
was so that mankind wouldn't fall off.

♦

God is a lousy landlord
in the wintertime—
no heat and no light.

♦

Diversity is God's way—
six billion humans who all
look and think very differently,
each with a song to sing.
The sum of all these songs
is God.

The Only Commandment

A friend said that there are only two
commandments that we must obey:
'Love God' and 'Love thy neighbor.'

So I said, 'If you love God but not your
neighbor, you'd be in trouble. But if you
loved your neighbor, you wouldn't have
to worry about loving God—that would
be the natural outcome.'

God expresses Himself
through our intuitive inner selves.

♦

Psychiatry reflects the norms of society,
cardiology the norms of God.

♦

Everyone knows the Devil is not perfect—
therefore, it must be assumed that
he will commit an occasional good deed.

♦

Prophets are the spume that ride
atop the wave of humankind.

The Pondering Jew

The Jewish mission is
summed up by the saying
'Think for yourself, schmuck.'

♦

Christianity is actually
a Jewish plot.

♦

The Jews believe that
the Messiah will come
when their work is done.
Christians believe that
the Messiah will come
and do their work for them.

♦

Christianity is the missionary
branch of Judaism.

To Be or Not to Be

If God had allowed Abraham to kill
his son, Isaac, He would have ended
the Jewish religion.

On the other hand, if He'd saved
His own son from crucifixion,
there never would have been Christianity.

It is not the Old Testament—
it's the Original Testament.

♦

A gentleman and a scholar
translates into Yiddish
as a *mentsch* and a *chockem*.

♦

When Abraham beseeched God
not to destroy Sodom and Gomorrah,
it was the first recorded case of hondling.

♦

It is not true that when Jews
use the term BCE, it means
'Before the Common Error.'

The Ten Lost Tribes

There are now 347 contenders
vying to be officially named one
of the Ten Lost Tribes of Israel.

Actually, the rumor that
Ten Lost Tribes ever existed
was a Jewish plot to make
other groups question their roots.

There never were *any* Lost Tribes.

Only insurance companies and Jews
know that God can do bad acts—
if He wants to.

♦

What would happen if all
of Christ's images showed Him
wearing a Star of David
around His neck?

♦

If Christians wish to study their
pagan past, they should look to the Jews.

♦

Jesus brought people back from the dead.
My job, as a doctor, is to stop them
from going there in the first place.

The Second Coming of Moses

In the late 1800s, architect John Roebling
designed and built the Brooklyn Bridge,
which connected Lower Manhattan
to the borough of Brooklyn.

By doing this, he freed the poor immi-
grant Jews from the tenement squalors on
the Lower East Side of Manhattan.

They escaped over the East River
by way of the Bridge—
to the *Promised Land* of Brooklyn.

The Mishnah says that if you find
a purse with a picture ID inside,
you must then return it.
If, however, you should find
a dollar bill with George
Washington's picture on it,
you can keep that, because
he ain't around anymore.

♦

If the cross fits, wear it.

♦

Mass marketing of
the Ten Commandments
was stalled until the
appearance of Christianity.

It is hard work
to live without idols.